What things can make you cheer up?

Kevin Hwu

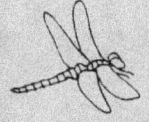

What things can make you cheer up?

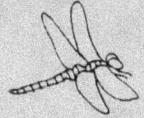

What things can make you cheer up?

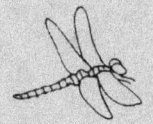

What things can make you cheer up ?

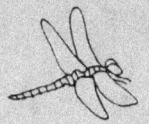 # What things can make you cheer up ?

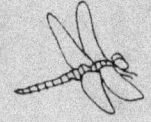

What things can make you cheer up?

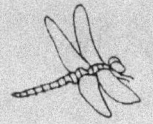

What things can
make you cheer up?

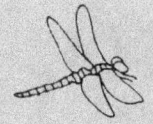

What things can make you cheer up?

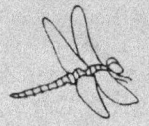

What things can make you cheer up ?

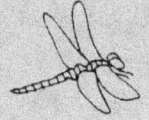

What things can make you cheer up?

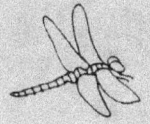

What things can make you cheer up?

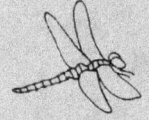 # What things can
make you cheer up?

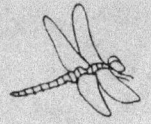 # What things can make you cheer up?

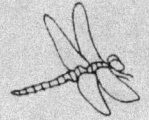

What things can make you cheer up?

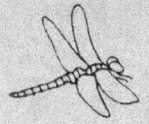

What things can
make you cheer up ?

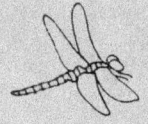

What things can make you cheer up?

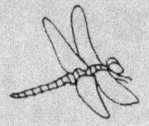

What things can make you cheer up?

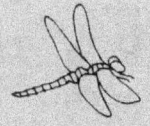 # What things can make you cheer up ?

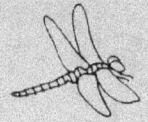
What things can make you cheer up?

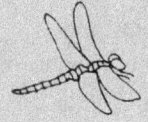

What things can make you cheer up ?

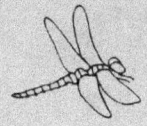

What things can make you cheer up?

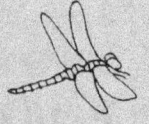# What things can
make you cheer up?

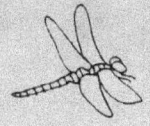

What things can make you cheer up ?

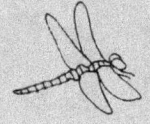# What things can
make you cheer up ?

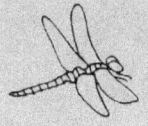

What things can make you cheer up?

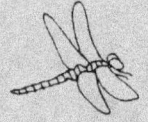

What things can make you cheer up?

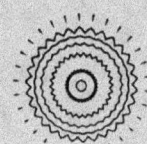

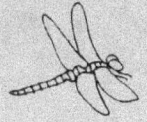

What things can
make you cheer up ?

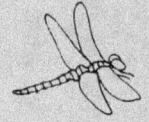

What things can make you cheer up?

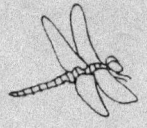

What things can make you cheer up?

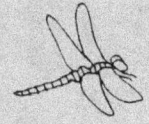

What things can make you cheer up?

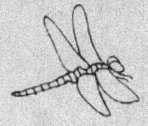

What things can make you cheer up ?

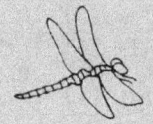

What things can make you cheer up ?

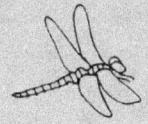 # What things can
make you cheer up ?

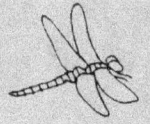
What things can make you cheer up?

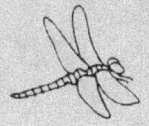

What things can make you cheer up ?

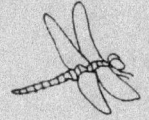

What things can make you cheer up?

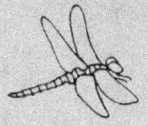

What things can make you cheer up?

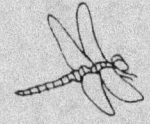

What things can
make you cheer up?

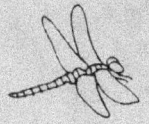

What things can make you cheer up?

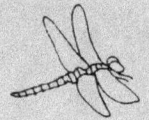

What things can make you cheer up ?

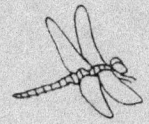 # What things can make you cheer up ?

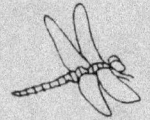# What things can
make you cheer up?

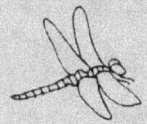

What things can
make you cheer up ?

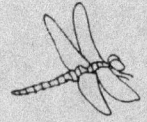

What things can make you cheer up ?

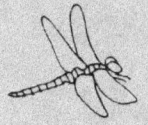

What things can
make you cheer up?

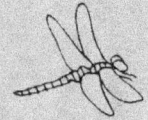

What things can make you cheer up ?

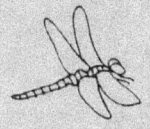# What things can
make you cheer up ?

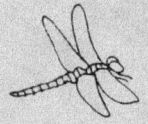 # What things can
make you cheer up ?

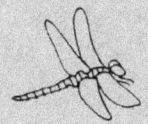

What things can make you cheer up ?

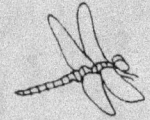

What things can make you cheer up?

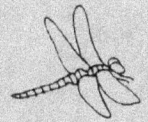 # What things can make you cheer up?

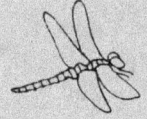

What things can
make you cheer up ?

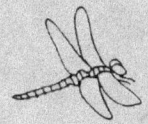 # What things can
make you cheer up ?

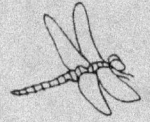# What things can
make you cheer up ?

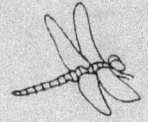

What things can
make you cheer up ?

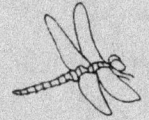

What things can make you cheer up?

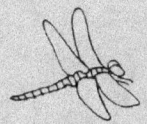

What things can make you cheer up?

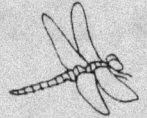

What things can make you cheer up?

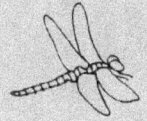 # What things can make you cheer up ?

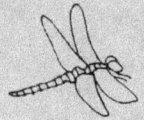

What things can make you cheer up?

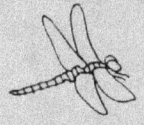

What things can
make you cheer up ?

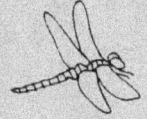

What things can
make you cheer up ?

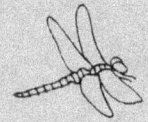

What things can make you cheer up?

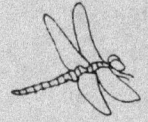

What things can make you cheer up ?

What things can
make you cheer up ?

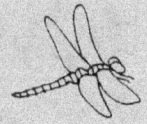

What things can
make you cheer up ?

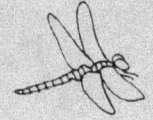

What things can make you cheer up?

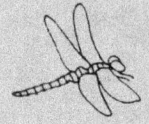

What things can make you cheer up ?

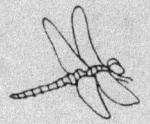 # What things can
make you cheer up?

 # What things can make you cheer up?

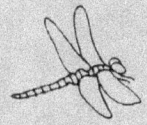

What things can make you cheer up ?

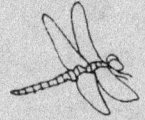

What things can make you cheer up ?

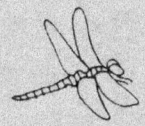

What things can make you cheer up?

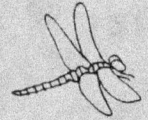

What things can make you cheer up ?

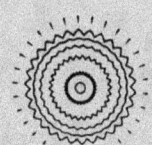

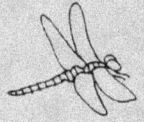

What things can make you cheer up ?

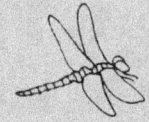

What things can make you cheer up ?

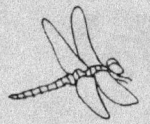

What things can make you cheer up?

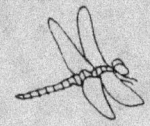

What things can make you cheer up?

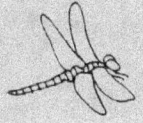

What things can
make you cheer up ?

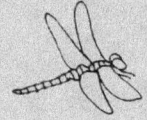

What things can make you cheer up?

What things can
make you cheer up?

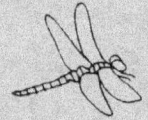

What things can make you cheer up?

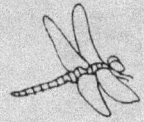

What things can make you cheer up?

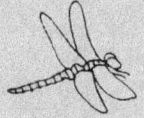

What things can make you cheer up ?

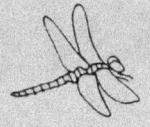 # What things can
make you cheer up ?

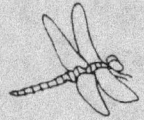

What things can make you cheer up?

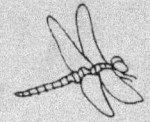

What things can
make you cheer up?

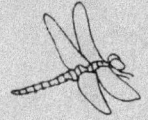

What things can make you cheer up?

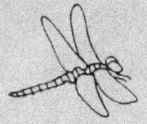

What things can make you cheer up?

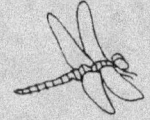# What things can
make you cheer up ?

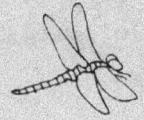

What things can make you cheer up?

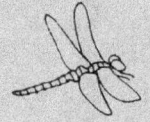

What things can
make you cheer up?

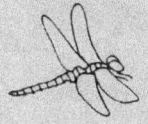

What things can make you cheer up?

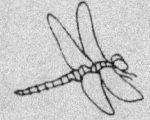

What things can make you cheer up ?

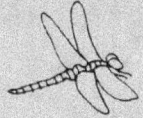

What things can make you cheer up?

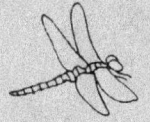 # What things can make you cheer up?

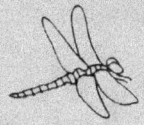

What things can make you cheer up?

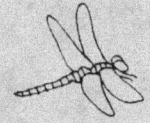 

What things can make you cheer up?

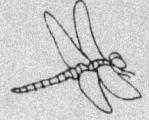

What things can make you cheer up?

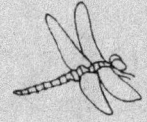

What things can make you cheer up?

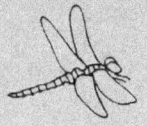

What things can make you cheer up?

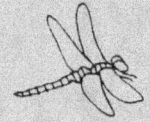 # What things can make you cheer up?

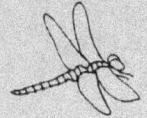

What things can
make you cheer up?

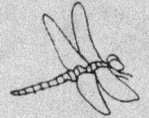

What things can make you cheer up?

What things can make you cheer up?

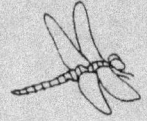

What things can
make you cheer up ?

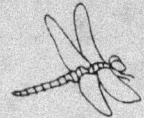

What things can
make you cheer up?

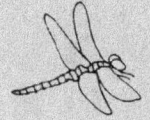 # What things can make you cheer up ?

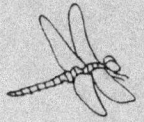

What things can make you cheer up?

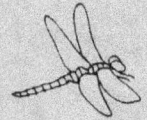

What things can
make you cheer up ?

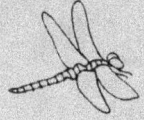

What things can make you cheer up?

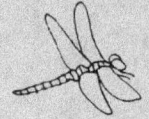 # What things can make you cheer up?

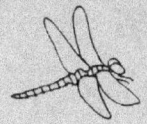

What things can
make you cheer up ?

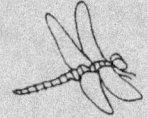

What things can make you cheer up ?

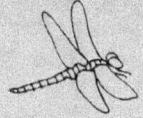

What things can
make you cheer up?

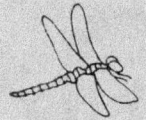

What things can make you cheer up ?

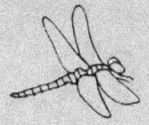

What things can make you cheer up?

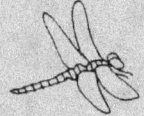# What things can
make you cheer up ?
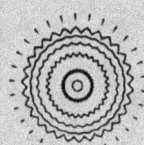

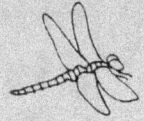

What things can make you cheer up?

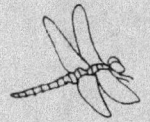

What things can make you cheer up?

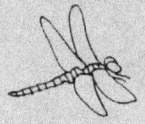

What things can make you cheer up?

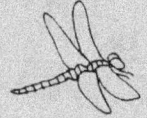

What things can make you cheer up ?

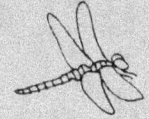

What things can
make you cheer up ?

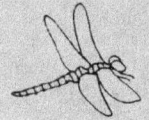 # What things can
make you cheer up?

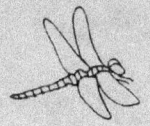

What things can
make you cheer up?

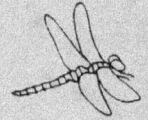

What things can make you cheer up ?

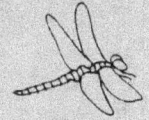 # What things can
make you cheer up?

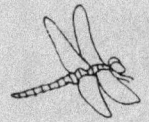

What things can make you cheer up ?

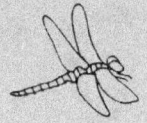

What things can make you cheer up?

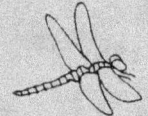 # What things can make you cheer up ?

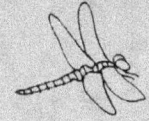 # What things can
make you cheer up?

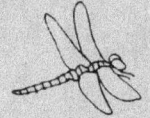

What things can make you cheer up?

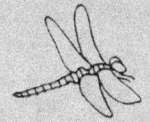

What things can make you cheer up?

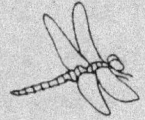

What things can make you cheer up?

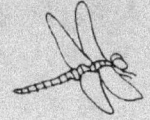# What things can
make you cheer up?

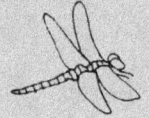 # What things can make you cheer up?

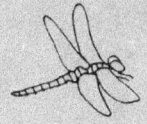

What things can
make you cheer up?

What things can make you cheer up ?

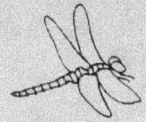

What things can
make you cheer up ?

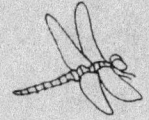

What things can make you cheer up?

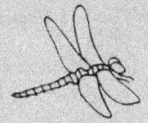

What things can
make you cheer up ?

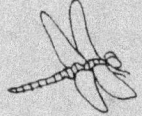
What things can make you cheer up?

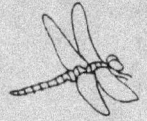

What things can make you cheer up?

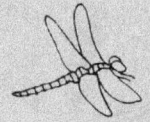

What things can
make you cheer up?

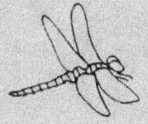

What things can make you cheer up?

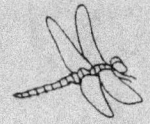 # What things can
make you cheer up ?

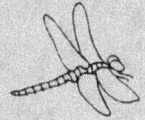

What things can make you cheer up?

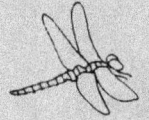# What things can make you cheer up ?

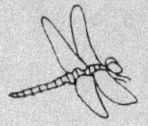

What things can
make you cheer up ?

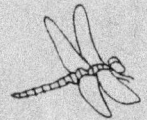

What things can
make you cheer up?

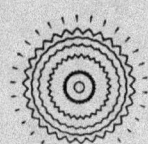

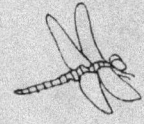 # What things can
make you cheer up?

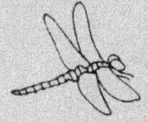

What things can make you cheer up ?

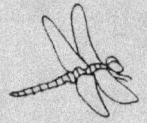

What things can
make you cheer up?

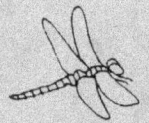 # What things can make you cheer up?

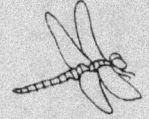

What things can make you cheer up?

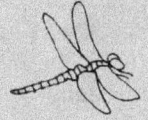 # What things can
make you cheer up ?

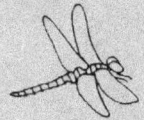

What things can make you cheer up?

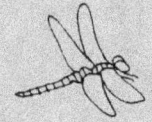

What things can make you cheer up ?

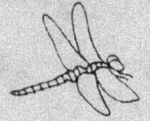# What things can
make you cheer up?

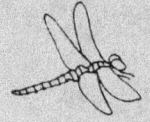 # What things can make you cheer up?

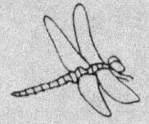

What things can make you cheer up?

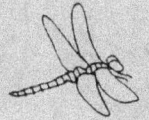

What things can make you cheer up?

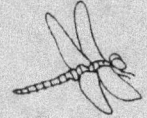

What things can make you cheer up?

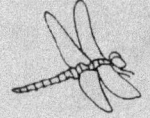

What things can make you cheer up?

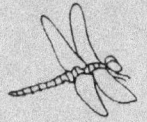

What things can make you cheer up ?

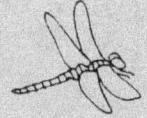

What things can make you cheer up?

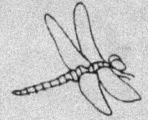

What things can make you cheer up?

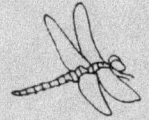# What things can
make you cheer up ?

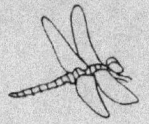 # What things can
make you cheer up ?

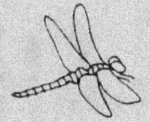

What things can make you cheer up ?

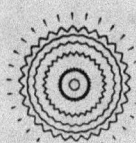

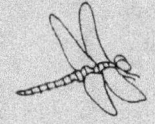

What things can make you cheer up?

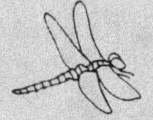

What things can
make you cheer up ?

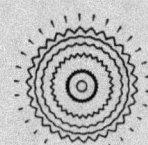

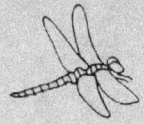

What things can make you cheer up ?

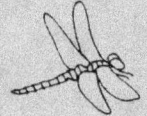
What things can make you cheer up?

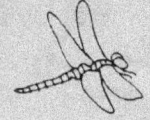

What things can make you cheer up?

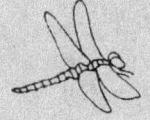 

What things can make you cheer up?

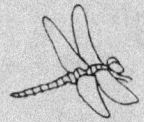

What things can make you cheer up?

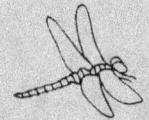

What things can
make you cheer up ?

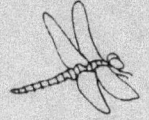

What things can
make you cheer up?

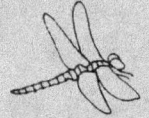

What things can make you cheer up?

www.ingramcontent.com/pod-product-compliance
Lightning Source LLC
Chambersburg PA
CBHW081723220526

45468CB00008B/1955